SHARKS!

A MY INCREDIBLE WORLD PICTURE BOOK

MY INCREDIBLE WORLD

Sharks are a type of fish that have been on Earth since before the dinosaurs — and even trees!

Sharks are found in almost every ocean and sea around the world.

They live in coastal areas, deep ocean waters, and coral reefs.

There are more than 500 different species of sharks — this one is called a **hammerhead**!

The largest species, the **whale shark**, grows to 40 feet (12 m) long, while the smallest is only 8 inches (20 cm)!

Sharks have a very powerful sense
of smell and could detect a drop
of blood in a swimming pool.

Some can even sense movement
and vibrations in the
water from miles away!

Sharks have several rows of teeth, and they continuously grow new teeth to replace the old ones that fall out!

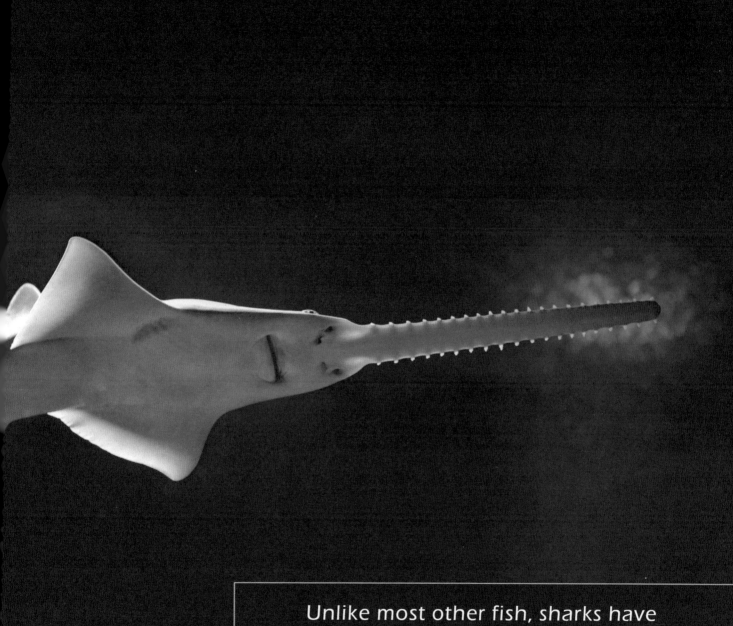

Unlike most other fish, sharks have skeletons that are made of **cartilage** instead of bones, just like your ears!

Sharks have a special sixth sense
called **electroreception**.

This sense allows them to detect the electrical signals given off by other animals!

Sharks are **carnivorous**, which means they only eat meat.

They feed on live prey like squid, mollusks, crustaceans, fish and some marine mammals.

Some sharks, like the **great white shark**, are apex predators, meaning they are at the top of the food chain.

A few can jump completely out of the water, a behavior called **breaching**, to catch prey or escape from danger.

Depending on the species,
sharks can swim up to 40 miles
per hour (64 kph)!

They are **ectothermic** (cold-blooded), which means their body temperature depends on their environment.

Sharks have **gills** on the sides of their bodies that allow them to breathe underwater.

Some little fish tag along with sharks, providing cleanup of parasites and food in exchange for the shark's protection!

Some sharks reproduce by laying eggs (**oviparous**) while others give birth to live young (**viviparous**).

Baby sharks are called **pups**!

Sharks are incredible!

Printed in Great Britain
by Amazon